D1808035

Living Safely in a Dangerous World:
Keys to Abiding in the Secret Place

Published by Mac Hammond Ministries a.k.a.,
Living Word Christian Center
© 1993, © 1996, © 2000, © 2003, © 2005
Living Word Christian Center

ISBN 1-57399-002-7

Mac Hammond Ministries
P.O. Box 29469
Minneapolis, MN 55429

Living Safely
in a
Dangerous World

Keys to Abiding
in the Secret Place

MAC HAMMOND

PART ONE

THE SECRET PLACE: A REFUGE OF SAFETY

Today, there is a message being screamed from every headline, television, radio, and magazine in the country. It's a message that can be summed up in a single word. DANGER!

Everywhere you turn, you are bombarded with horror stories. Innocent bystanders are cut down in drive-by shootings. On a regular basis, children are being snatched and subjected to the unspeakable. And the threat of worldwide terrorism hangs like a heavy pal over the earth. In addition to that, it seems even the elements are out to get us.

Experts tell us we should be concerned about ultraviolet and electromagnetic radiation giving us cancer. Contaminated water, air, and food are worries for many. Others wonder if the health-care worker currently treating them is carrying the AIDS virus.

If this weren't enough cause for alarm, according to some "experts," western civilization's entire system of banking and finance could collapse at any moment, plunging us into the next dark age.

Given this barrage of impending doom and disaster, is it any wonder more Americans than ever suffer under record levels of anxiety and fear?

In the process, we've become increasingly isolated behind barred windows, high-tech security systems, and vicious dogs. We're ever on our guard. Ever watchful. Always suspicious. Sadly, this is often as true for Christians as it is for unbelievers.

Many have come to believe that living in fear is simply part of life in the 21st century. If you're one of them, I've got startling news for you. You don't have to live that way. Some believers have discovered a way to live in absolute peace and safety. They've found an invincible shield of protection far more powerful than any security system.

They know beyond a doubt that no violence, disease, or disaster can touch them in a lasting or harmful way. They lie down in peace and arise in confidence.

Who are these fearless ones? Those who have discovered the key to living in the "Secret Place" of God. But this is not a select or divinely favored group. You can join them. Any believer can. In the next few pages, I'll take you to God's Word and show you how.

Moses' Song of Safety

In the 91st chapter of Psalms, we find a remarkable set of verses. Whereas most of the psalms came from the pen of King David (by inspiration of the Holy Ghost, of course), this is one of the psalms of Moses. He wrote it during the 40 years the nation of Israel was wandering in the wilderness.

Those long years in that hostile, barren wilderness gave Moses a special understanding and appreciation of God's divine protection. Without it, the people he'd been called to lead wouldn't have survived a week. He'd seen water spring from a rock, food fall from heaven, and shoes that didn't wear out, even after decades of walking over rough terrain.

He'd seen seas part and the greatest army of his day destroyed in a single hour. He had experienced deliverance from hostile tribes and wild animals. He had been guided through unknown territory by a pillar of fire sent from the very throne of God Himself. Yes, Moses knew a little bit about the protecting hand of God over His servants.

The 91st Psalm is born of Moses' personal experience with God the Deliverer. Notice the first verse:

He that dwelleth in the secret place of the most High shall abide under the shadow of the Almighty.

Immediately Moses tells us of a special place he calls "the secret place of the most High." We're told it is possible to "dwell" there. The Hebrew word translated "dwell" literally means, *to stake a claim to or to remain.*

The Secret Place of God is not a place you can slip in and out of from hour to hour. It's not a position that is attained one moment and lost another. No, to truly abide in the Secret Place requires living there. It's a lifestyle.

What is the result of living in this Secret Place? The second half of the verse tells us you "shall abide under the shadow of the Almighty." Does God really cast a shadow? He may, but that's not what this verse is talking about.

Throughout the Bible, the concept of a shadow is used to symbolize God's anointing and covering presence.

In Luke 1:35, we're told the Holy Spirit "overshadowed" Mary when she conceived the Son of God, Jesus. In Luke 9:34, we're told a cloud "overshadowed" Peter, James, and John when they were with Jesus on the Mount of Transfiguration. In both cases, a shadow typifies the presence and power of God coming into contact with human flesh.

When you dwell in the Secret Place of almighty God, you are covered with His power, presence, and anointing. And as we've seen, it's not just an occasional thing. You live there.

Ask yourself, "What would such a person's attitude be toward life? With what mindset would they face the day?" Verse two gives us the answer.

I will say of the Lord, He is my refuge and my fortress: my God; in him will I trust.

When a person is living in the Secret Place, he or she can't help but proclaim the fact of God's protection. Not every believer makes this kind of declaration, however. More often than not, instead of hearing "God is my refuge from trouble," you'll hear, "God is giving me trouble."

Many sincere Christians believe God has allowed them to get sick, experience disaster, or face hardship, because He wants to teach them something. They don't see God as their shelter from calamity. They see Him as the source of it!

These people are strangers to the Secret Place. Tragically, most don't even know it exists.

A Place of Deliverance

Moses certainly didn't buy into the old "God is making me sick to teach me something" myth. Of the person dwelling in the Secret Place, he declares:

> *Surely he shall deliver thee from the snare of the fowler, and from the noisome pestilence.* (Psalm 91:3)

In biblical times, the fowler was a person who had trained a hawk or other bird of prey to go out, kill, and retrieve an animal. The fowler literally hunted game with these deadly birds.

Here, the fowler is used as a metaphor for Satan, the enemy of our soul. The Bible frequently refers to him as a predator. Peter said, "Be sober, be vigilant; because your adversary the devil, as a roaring lion, walketh about, seeking whom he may devour." (I Peter 5:8)

Satan has some deadly traps set for the unwary believer. Moses is saying that the person who abides in the Secret Place will not fall prey to these snares of the enemy. Then he goes on to include deliverance from the "noisome pestilence." That's a fancy King James way of translating the Hebrew phrase *havvah deber*. It literally means "onrushing calamity or plague."

We've seen some pretty devastating examples of onrushing calamities in this nation, with terrorism topping the list. In addition to that, we've experienced plagues, hurricanes, tornadoes, earthquakes, and terrible floods. To the average person, these are enormously frightful events. But not for the dwellers in the Secret Place. They rest in the calm assurance that "surely" they will be delivered when disaster suddenly strikes.

How well protected is the believer who abides under the shadow of the almighty God? According to verse four, he is covered by the "wings" of God Himself.

> *He shall cover thee with his feathers, and under his wings shalt thou trust: his truth shall be thy shield and buckler.*

Of course, the Word isn't suggesting that God literally has wings and feathers. Once again, Moses uses a metaphor to show in word pictures how secure this believer truly is.

In nature, when a storm arises, adult eagles with eaglets in the nest will go gather the helpless birds and blanket them securely under their wings. Under the protecting span of those powerful pinions, the tiny birds are so protected from the effects of the storm they may not even be aware that one is blowing.

This is the image the Holy Spirit wants us to grasp. When the storms of life blow, God's desire is to cover His children with His wings and keep them safe. It is His true heart's desire. You can trust those wings. But this haven of protection is only available in the Secret Place.

Protection From Violence

The second half of the above verse talks about God's truth being "a shield and buckler." This uses military equipment to represent two different types of protection available to the believer.

Obviously, the "truth" referred to here is God's Word. There is no other standard of truth. Jesus, the living Word, said "I am the Way, the Truth, and the Life."

A soldier in Bible times would use his shield to protect himself from a flurry of arrows or spears. It represents a source of protection from large or numerous threats.

The buckler, on the other hand, was a protection which was strapped around the wrist. It was small and light and, therefore, ideal for quickly fending off or blocking small attacks from single arrows.

God's Word offers both kinds of protection. Immerse yourself in it and it will provide protection from any size or type of assault the enemy may launch against you. His truth will be your shield and buckler.

Freedom From Fear

Once you begin to realize the strength, diversity, and comprehensiveness of God's protection in the Secret Place, the obvious result is peace. With God overshadowing and covering you with His wings and with His truth as your shield and buckler, nothing in this earth can make you afraid. That's precisely the psalmist's next point.

> *Thou shalt not be afraid for the terror by night; nor for the arrow that flieth by day; nor for the pestilence that walketh in darkness; nor for the destruction that wasteth at noonday.* (v.5, 6)

These verses describe two different types of attacks. One that comes at night—it can't be seen—and one that comes in broad daylight—you see it coming. In the Secret Place, you won't be afraid of either one of them.

No matter which type of attack the enemy tries against you—the full, frontal assault or the blind-siding sneak attack—you will not fear them.

This freedom from fear is important. Why? Because fear actually acts as a magnet in the spiritual realm to attract the very things you fear. Job discovered this truth and exclaimed, "For the thing which I greatly feared is come upon me, and that which I was afraid of is come unto me." (Job 3:25)

Fear often becomes a type of self-fulfilling prophecy. Take, for example, a woman who is preoccupied with the prospect of getting cancer. She studies up on it. She talks about it. She fears it. Then one awful day she gets the report from her doctor. That which she has greatly feared has come upon her.

You can understand why this is so, when you realize fear is the reciprocal of faith. Faith is your belief in God's power and desire to do good in your life. Fear is your belief in Satan's power to do you harm.

Just as faith activates God to bring the good things for which you are believing, fear activates and looses Satan to bring the very things you fear. This is why it is vital that you learn to abide in the Secret Place of God. For only when you are free from fear are you truly in a place where the enemy can't touch you.

A thousand shall fall at thy side, and ten thousand at thy right hand; but it shall not come nigh thee. Only with thine eyes shalt thou behold and see the reward of the wicked. (v.7, 8)

I can't read these verses without thinking back to some things I experienced as a pilot in Vietnam. I am particularly reminded of a fellow pilot I knew. He was a committed Pentecostal Christian who knew how to stand on the Word of God.

For him, the words "A thousand shall fall at thy side, and ten thousand at thy right hand; but it shall not come nigh thee" were never far from his lips. He lived them and breathed them. More importantly, he believed them. He honestly did not believe he could be hurt.

This man flew over 250 combat missions in an F100 providing hazardous close air support for our troops on the ground. He was one of the most decorated pilots of the war, and although he saw many of his comrades wounded or killed, he never received so much as a scratch.

I've known infantry soldiers who came through the bloodiest battles of the war unharmed by standing on this verse. In some cases, they were part of only a tiny handful of survivors. Even in a hail of bullets, these men knew how to abide in the Secret Place.

Notice something else about these verses. The thousands who are falling are "at thy side" and "at thy right hand." These aren't people who are far away and distant from you. They are your Christian brothers and sisters—those who are born again but aren't abiding in the Secret Place.

Many believers get tripped up, because they see another believer become the victim of disaster or tragedy. They think, *Gosh, they love God, if it could happen to them, it could happen to me!*

Loving God or being a good Christian has nothing to do with it. The only thing that is going to offer you the level of safety we're talking about is learning to abide in the Secret Place.

But how? you may be wondering. *I can see in the Word the Secret Place is where I want to be! But how do I get there?* Read on to find out.

PART TWO

LIVING IN THE SECRET PLACE

Imagine yourself surrounded by an impenetrable wall of protection. Picture yourself enveloped by an invisible force field no sickness, injury, or evil can penetrate. Does that sound too good to be true? That level of security is no fantasy. It's the Secret Place. And it's precisely where God wants you to live.

In the first section of this book, we began an exploration of what the psalmist Moses called "the secret place" in Psalm 91. "He that dwelleth in the secret place of the most High shall abide under the shadow of the Almighty." (v.1) There we saw that abiding in the Secret Place was actually a state of living in which the believer enjoys absolute protection from all evil.

We also saw how precious few Christians ever enter this blessed refuge of safety. According to verse seven, only one in thousands ever finds the Secret Place. Yet God clearly states His earnest desire that all His children dwell there.

You may be thinking, *Surely finding the Secret Place must be a complex, mysterious thing available only to super-Christians!* On the contrary, abiding in the shelter of God's protection is startlingly simple. And it's accessible to even the newest of believers.

Of course, "simple" doesn't mean easy. If abiding in the Secret Place was a piece of cake, more of God's people would be enjoying this extraordinary level of security. Still, those who know the key to entering this fortress of peace, reap rewards most Christians only dream of.

The Key to the Secret Place

Simply stated, the Secret Place is a place of fellowship with God. When you are in a place of close fellowship with your heavenly Father, you're "abiding in the shadow of the Almighty." Perhaps you'd already guessed that. Yet, I almost hesitate to use the term "fellowship" to describe this level of relationship with God. The word has been so overused in Christian circles that it has almost become meaningless.

The type of fellowship I'm talking about refers to deep, intimate friendship. Achieving this level of intimacy with God requires more than simply attending church regularly. It demands more than an occasional "quickie quiet time" in the morning.

No, abiding in the Secret Place does not come cheaply, but it is possible. Otherwise, God wouldn't have told us it was available. It's just that most of us don't want it badly enough to pay the price.

You may be thinking, *I don't have to go through all that. I'll just read Psalm 91 and receive it by faith!* It doesn't work that way, my friend. These benefits don't come by faith. They come by fellowship. They are a natural byproduct of constant, intimate relationship with your heavenly Father.

Sure, faith is involved. But you're not going to have the faith necessary to receive this level of protection outside of fellowship with the Lord. Only when God is your ever-present companion will you be able to lay claim to the promises of the Secret Place.

"But how, Pastor Mac? How do I enter into a close, personal relationship with someone I can't see, hear, or touch?"

Don't despair. It's not as difficult as it may sound. The Bible gives you some clear and simple steps you can take for developing a rich, deep, and exciting relationship with God.

Read All About It

Do you remember the wording of the first verse of Psalm 91?

He that dwelleth in the secret place of the most High shall abide under the shadow of the Almighty.

The words "dwell" and "abide" mean very much the same thing. To dwell or abide in a place means to live there continually.

One key to living in the Secret Place is "abiding" in God's Word. This is precisely what

Jesus meant when He said, "If ye abide in me, and my words abide in you, you shall ask what ye will, and it shall be done unto you." (John 15:7)

If you're serious about getting to a place in which you live each day in the safety of the Secret Place, your first step is to immerse yourself in the Word of God. That means serious, concentrated Bible study.

Spend enough time abiding in the Word and it will eventually begin abiding in you. How do you know you've reached that point? When your first response to any situation is to speak the Word. When you're asked a question—out comes the Word. When you're faced with a problem—speaking the Word is your instinctive response.

It is unavoidable. When circumstances start putting the squeeze on you, the stuff that fills your heart will come out of your mouth. Think about it. When the pressure is on, what is the first thing out of your mouth? Is it the standard, cliche junk everyone else says? Or is it what God's Word has to say about the situation?

That is how you know if you've been abiding in the Word and it has been abiding in you. Jesus was very clear on this point.

Out of the abundance of the heart the mouth speaketh. (Matthew 12:34)

It is by missing this crucial first step that many believers fail to enter the safety of the Secret Place. Bible study alone, however, will not produce the level of intimacy with God required to dwell there. Another dimension must be added.

Let's Talk

You can find out a lot about someone just by reading his letters. But there is a certain level of friendship that can only be developed through many hours of face to face, personal contact. The same is true of relationship with God.

If all you ever do is read God's letters (the Bible), you will never truly know Him in the depth and detail of a true friend. It is only in the prayer closet that you will discover God's personality, His character, His methods, and His love. Nowhere else can you plumb the depths of your Father's mercy or explore the riches of His wisdom.

Through the Bible, you can know God as Savior, Lord, King, and Deliverer. But only through prayer can you truly know Him as friend.

In Psalm 103 we're told, "He [God] made known his ways unto Moses, his acts unto the children of Israel." (v.7) This describes two different levels of relationship with God. The children of Israel knew about God. They knew what He had done. But Moses knew God's ways.

How did Moses develop this deeper knowledge of God? By spending time with Him!

> *And the Lord spake unto Moses face to face*
> *as a man speaketh unto a friend.*
> (Exodus 33:11)

In Old Testament times, this level of access to God was limited to prophets on mountaintops and priests in the Holy of Holies. But now, every believer can know God in this extraordinary way—just as Moses did!

> *Therefore, brethren, since we have full freedom and confidence to enter into the [Holy of] Holies,...Let us all come forward and draw near with true (honest and sincere) hearts in unqualified assurance and absolute conviction engendered by faith... having our hearts sprinkled and purified from a guilty (evil) conscience and our bodies cleansed with pure water.*
> (Hebrews 10:19-22 Amp.)

Think of it! You have been granted unlimited, personal access to the Creator of the universe. Even more mind boggling is the knowledge that He desires your company. He wants you to know Him as intimate friend.

Push for the Breakthrough

The question remains: If God's offer of friendship and communion is so wonderful and free, why do so few Christians ever move into this level of relationship?

I believe the answer is that most believers give up in discouragement before they ever get a taste of it. Many new Christians hear about the joys of experiencing God in a quiet time and want to get in on it. With high hopes, they start having a regular time of Bible study and prayer. But when they don't experience fireworks, a cloud of glory, or an audible voice from heaven right away, they simply quit in frustration.

The truth is, it takes perseverance, patience, and consistency to develop an intimate walk with God. And while there are exceptions, for most of us, it is very much a journey of faith in the early stages. It certainly was for me.

When Lynne and I first started walking wholeheartedly with the Lord, I would get discouraged when I compared my devotional life with her's. Here I was, striving and straining to get into the Word and press into God's presence yet coming away with absolutely no sense of fellowship with God. Lynne, on the other hand, seemed to be able to simply close her eyes and be transported into a glorious rendezvous with heaven.

I would wonder, at times, if there was something wrong with me. Still, I continued to press into God's presence though I got no discernible results. Then one morning I awakened to find my room filled with the presence and glory of the Lord. At that moment, He was more real to me than my wife lying beside me.

You, too, will experience a breakthrough in this area if you don't grow weary in well doing. Stay in the Word of God. Stay constant in prayer. It may take weeks, months, or even years, but you will achieve a breakthrough if you will stay with it.

The day will come when the accumulated force of all your prayer and praise will propel you into an entirely new dimension in your relationship with God. It will be that proverbial "quantum leap" forward.

Sadly, the vast majority of believers quit before they ever reach that glorious point. This is doubly tragic, because it's the very point at which you're ready to start learning to abide in the Secret Place. To do so, you simply practice the presence of God on a moment-by-moment basis. The result? You go through your day in constant communion with Him.

That doesn't mean you walk around in some kind of spiritual daze. In reality, you're sharper, more discerning, and more sensitive to what's going on around you than ever before. It's just that you now are so connected to the Spirit and His voice that you are able to hear His promptings, warnings, and instructions. It is truly a wonderful way to live!

This is also where you really begin to be able to put away the old desires of your fleshly nature. Jesus-in-you becomes such a solid reality to you, it changes what you do and say.

You'll think, *How could I possibly take Jesus with me into that sinful situation?* You'll cringe at the thought of uttering a word that would bring dishonor to Him.

As your actions change, the "old man" of the flesh begins passing away and the "newness of life" that is yours in Christ begins to emerge.

Just don't get the cart before the horse. Before you begin trying to implement every principle and guideline you see in the Word, you must first have developed a vital, tangible relationship with Jesus Christ. I'm talking about a relationship that is more intimate than your most intimate human relationship.

Then and only then, are you ready to start implementing all the things you see in God's Word.

Do you want to abide in the Secret Place? Do you want to experience the kind of supernatural protection from evil that Moses described so vividly in the 91st Psalm? Then purpose in your heart to spend time in the Word, in prayer, and in praise. Follow through with consistency and patience.

Take these steps and before you know it, you'll not only call the Lord "God," you'll also call Him "friend." When that becomes a daily reality in your life, you'll be living in a realm where no evil can enter—the Secret Place of the Most High.

Conclusion

Imagine life without fear. Picture yourself doing the things God has called you to do without a trace of anxiety or worry. It's not a religious pipe dream. It's not only for an elite class of Christians. It's a reality called the Secret Place of the most high God and you belong there. It's part of your inheritance as a child of God.

Begin familiarizing yourself with the many wonderful protections of the Secret Place by repeating this confession based on the Amplified translation of Psalm 91.

I dwell in the secret place of the Most High and remain stable and fixed under the shadow of the Almighty, whose power no foe can withstand. I will say of the Lord, He is my refuge and my fortress, my God on Him I lean and rely and in Him I confidently trust.

For then He will deliver me from the snare of the fowler and from the deadly pestilence. Then He will cover me with His pinions and under His wings shall I trust and find refuge.

His truth and His faithfulness are a shield and a buckler. I shall not be afraid of the terror of the night nor of the arrow, the evil plots and slanders of the wicked that flies by day, nor of the pestilence that stalks in darkness, nor of the destruction and sudden death that surprise and lay waste at noonday.

A thousand may fall at my side and ten thousand at my right hand, but it shall not come near me. Only a spectator shall I be inaccessible in the secret place of the Most High as I witness the reward of the wicked.

*Because I have made the Lord my refuge,
and the Most High my dwelling place,
there shall no evil befall me nor any plague
or calamity come near my tent, for He will
give His angels especial charge over me to
accompany, defend and preserve me in
all my ways of obedience and service. They
shall bear me up on their hands lest I dash
my foot against a stone. I shall tread upon
a lion and adder, the young lion and the
serpent shall I trample under foot. Because
I have set my love upon Him, therefore
He will deliver me. He will set me on
high because I know and understand His
Name, I have personal knowledge of His
mercy, love and kindness, I trust and rely
on Him knowing He will never forsake
me, no never.*

*I shall call upon Him and He will
answer me. He will be with me in trouble.
He will deliver me and honor me. With
long life will He satisfy me and show me
His salvation.*

Prayer for Salvation

God in heaven, I come to You in the name of Jesus. I confess that I have not lived my life for You. But I'm glad to know I can change that. I've decided to believe that Jesus is Your son, and that He died on the cross and rose again from the dead, so I might have eternal life and the blessings of life now. Jesus, come into my heart, be my Savior and be my Lord. From this day forward and to the best of my ability, I'll live my life for You. In Jesus' name I pray. Amen.

If you prayed this prayer, it is important to share this with someone. We would consider it an honor for you to share this important decision with us.

ABOUT THE AUTHOR

Mac Hammond is senior pastor of Living Word Christian Center, a large and growing body of Christian believers in Brooklyn Park (a suburb of Minneapolis), Minnesota. He is the host of the Winner's Way broadcast and author of several internationally distributed books. Mac is broadly acclaimed for his ability to apply the principles of the Bible to practical situations and the challenges of daily living.

Mac Hammond graduated from Virginia Military Institute in 1965 with a Bachelor's degree in English. Upon graduation, he entered the Air Force with a regular officer's commission and reported for pilot training at Moody Air Force Base in Georgia. He received his wings in November 1966, and subsequently served two tours of duty in Southeast Asia, accumulating 198 combat missions. He was honorably discharged in 1970 with the rank of Captain.

Between 1970 and 1980, Mac was involved in varying capacities in the general aviation industry including ownership of a successful air cargo business serving the Midwestern United States. A business merger brought the Hammonds to Minneapolis where they ultimately founded Living Word Christian Center in 1980 with 12 people in attendance. After almost 25 years, that group of twelve people has grown into an active church body of 9,000 members. Today some of the outreaches that spring from Living Word include Maranatha Christian Academy, a fully-accredited, pre-K through 12th grade Christian school; Maranatha College, an evening and weekend college with an uncompromising Christian environment; Living Free Recovery Services, a state licensed outpatient treatment facility for chemical dependency; Club 3 Degrees, a cutting-edge Christian music club which is smoke/alcohol free; The Compassion Center, a multi-faceted outreach to inner-city residents; CFAITH, an online cooperative missionary outreach of hundreds of national and international organizations providing faith-based content and a nonprofit family oriented ISP; and a national and international media outreach that includes hundreds of audio/video teaching series, the *Winner's Way* broadcast, the *PrayerNotes* publication, and *Winner's Way* magazine.

Water, Wind & Fire: Understanding the New Birth and the Baptism of the Holy Spirit

Who God Is Not: Exploding the Myths About His Nature and His Ways

Winning the World: Becoming the Bold Soul Winner God Created You to Be

Books by Lynne Hammond

The Master Is Calling: Discovering the Wonders of Spirit-Led Prayer

The Spiritual Enrichment Series (four books by Lynne, recently retitled)

When It's Time for a Miracle: The Hour of Impossible Breakthroughs Is Now!

Staying Faith: How to Stand Until the Answer Arrives

Heaven's Power for the Harvest: Be Part of God's End-Time Spiritual Outpouring

Living in God's Presence: Receive Joy, Peace, and Direction in the Secret Place of Prayer

Renewed in His Presence: Satisfying Your Hunger for God

When Healing Doesn't Come Easily

Secrets to Powerful Prayer: Discovering the Languages of the Heart

Dare to Be Free!

The Table of Blessing: Recipes From the Family and Friends of Living Word Christian Center

Book by Mac & Lynne Hammond

Keys to Compatibility: Opening the Door to a Marvelous Marriage

For more information about this ministry or a complete catalog of teaching tapes and other materials available, please write:

Mac Hammond Ministries
P.O. Box 29469
Minneapolis, MN 55429-2946

mac-hammond.org